Voices on the Corner

Voices on the Corner

Harold J. Recinos

RESOURCE *Publications* · Eugene, Oregon

VOICES ON THE CORNER

Resource Publications
An Imprint of Wipf and Stock Publishers
199 W. 8th Ave., Suite 3
Eugene, OR 97401

www.wipfandstock.com

ISBN 13: 978-1-4982-2902-9

Manufactured in the U.S.A.   10/09/2015

Acknowledgements

Grateful acknowledgement is made to Westminster John Knox Press and Abingdon Press in which some of my poems have appeared.

Excerpted from Jesus Weeps, Published by Abingdon Press (c) 1992.Used by permission. All rights reserved.

Latino Town
Been Waiting
14th Street

Excerpted from Who Comes in the Name of the Lord? Published by Abingdon Press (c) 1997.Used by permission. All rights reserved.

Burning in Heaven
The Witness
The Crucified

Excerpted from Good News from the Barrio: Prophetic Witness for the Church (c) 2006. Used by Permission. All rights reserved.

Suspects
Games
The Church
Piece Work

Excerpted from Harold J. Recinos and Hugo Magallanes, eds. Jesus in the Hispanic Community: Images of Christ from Theology to Popular Religion (c)2009.

The Water
The Kiss
Speak

Finally, this book was made possible by support from Perkins School of Theology's Center for the Study of Latino/a Christianity and Religions, and funds provided by the Henry Luce Foundation.

Contents

Contents

King

the night falls into
brightly colored light

that streams down the
mountain passes, rolls

along the city streets and
touches people he never

knew, while each radiant
moment turns hate into stone

with the weight of simple
words that tell the truth.

beloved, you the people in
King's dream, the sadness in

his daily gaze, the immense
travail deeply felt that steered

his step along a different
path, must echo now the

righteous dream. shout
even in the places you

cannot reach, scream on
this road so long ago begun

the magnificent sound of
free at last, free at last.

The Walk

we came this way before
afraid of the dark, looking up
at the stars that know nothing

of what lies ahead, or a world
in need of heaven, or the cries
on all the corners, or the need

to make truth out of all the
faulty things that make our
trembling self. we came this

way before frightened by the
falling tears left by people utterly
against the loud voices that quarrel

on the sidewalk and drag us into
their empty pits. we came this way
before hoping to find light lingering

some place not yet seen that calls
us over to it.

The Cathedral

they depart the Cathedral
feeling history not their own,
touched by the mysterious

grace that made your church
a foe of money, military
and might. each day they

come to pray for you,
the pastor who dared
to speak the long view

of a new promised land
in a time of sorrow and
death. they come to the

Cathedral to stand even now
beside you recalling those who
bathed the earth with blood

could not stop you from
resurrecting to guide them.
daily they come to look

upon you more certain now
of the meaning of love and
the magnificence of the God

who never left you.

Games

I saw children playing
on the corner wearing
the smiles old prayers

often bid for the whole
block. abuelitas came
out of tired buildings

to sit on stoops tying
unlaced sneakers with
wrinkled hands made

before time. they looked
up smiling at the old
man with stories that

cough up on all the
corners loud enough
to raise blinds and

open eyes in all the
windows. kids who
think games never

end made the street
sing a babble of
fun that left imprints

on the crowds on the
well-kept sidewalks.
we drew nearer to the

truth that sabado
afternoon simply
to drink it still.

The Water

when the city was
new to me faces

smiled on all the
corners, the fire

hydrants in summer
opened, kids undid

cans at each end
for water games,

skinny old men ran
through puddles, bag

carrying abuelas laughed
in rainbow vapors, wet

kids ran to bodegas
with nickels in hand

for five cookies, records
played loud music

on Saturday, domino
games were unending,

girls jumped roped,
the church bells kept

time, nights were not
wounded by fear, we

believed, loved, lived,
with such risa, and there

were no strangers.

Speak

I sit and hear
about the man
from Guatemala

shot last week
by cops who never
sob about wrong

doing. I see
bony children in
unlit apartments

neglected, abused,
desperately crying
in beaten mothers'

arms. I hear people
talk about martyrs, agony
without end, the death

of the world, the vain
cries everywhere, the
churches unable to see

and hear beyond their
sullen Sabbath. I dwell
on the silence of God.

The Place

we have come
into the church

after years of death
lived in a world

no longer listening
to God. the incense

cleanses our wounds
as flickering candles

on a crystal moon night
carry us to you. we sit

before two sore eyes
on a saint never suspicious
of strangers, full of acceptance,

sleeplessly waiting, and find
rest. we light candles for those

turned dusty ash to raise
them once again from the

terrible silence.

The Drowning

you walked across
the bridge far, far
away to the screaming

dock that assembled
the people with candles
flickering into the

night beside the
lady whose five year
old drowned. you saw

them speak in tongues
and cast cries to an
invisible God who never

misses funerals. you
watched them pull the
little girl from the

river that kept her
for three days cursing
all the horror. you

fell beside the child's
mother who snapped in
the company of strangers

her tears carried by
a desolate wind.

The Street

have you walked the
avenue where sidewalks
turn red, and tenement

windows never open.
one evening I fell
beside a motherless

friend shot in the
head for selling baby
powder to dope fiends

who had dried blood
mixed with rage on
veins craving a fix.

death came to life
on this street the
pious only swallow

with prayer, never
minding the drowning
sorrow of those only

strong enough to sob
in God's city for the pale
and sudden departures.

will you walk a bit
further into the corner
night, where the people

gather in store front
faith to speak prayers
before the dropping

darkness, where no one
sees us hunger, or thirst
or reach for life beyond

the ascending coffins
and tolling bells.

Piety Lost

that church piety you
claim to build life
closer to God on

earth has never
more weakly felt
the horrors that

parade each day
in front of us
as kids are killed

by errant cops
in a world that
easily unnamed

the evil your belief
once declared so
real. the spectacle

of such numbing pain
now only makes you
stutter that salvation

is God's plan for us.
such piety must know
the sobbing will not

end should it ever
come . . .

Latino Town

merengue music is being tapped
rhythmically by tired work feet,
drenching the hot sidewalk in sweat:

it's Latino town and the secondhand
cars, the third and fourth ones too,
are up on jacks being fixed and admired.

it doesn't make a difference on a sabado
afternoon. it's Latino town and grandmothers
are emerging from the tenements adopting whole

blocks, silently being everyone's abuelita.
it's Latino town and the hydrants are at full force;
scattered cans of Coke and beer are being

gathered by little children,
who run up to the old man selling piragua
to ask that he open the ends so they can spray

the water at each other, the buses, the
buildings and have a laugh, such a risa.
it's Latino town and at ten o'clock this morning

the Goya little league will begin to play against
Bustelo's little league, and it's beans against cafe
once again, they say. it's Latino town and Julia

and Tito have opened their first-floor window
real wide listening to the music they put on la
radiola while rehearsing the moves for tonight's big

baile. it's Latino town and in front of the bodega
sit Don Carlo, Don Pepe, Don Wilfredo, and Charly
on milk boxes emptied of treats, playing dominoes.

it's Latino town, and all the smiles are in
Spanish. . . .

Madness

gazing into the distance,
the wind pressing against
our shoulders, the black

crows thickly flock in the
darkness of a world strutting

intolerance of difference in
an endless season of religious

madness. in the procession
of the dead, the hell hung for

us by pious killers for view
in the bloody public squares,

speak the end. under this
threatening cloud lives

whisper through the deafening
silence stories of unrecognizable

human beings who mount truth
with violence in the name of

blood-spilling Gods. you born
beneath the bright enormous star,

why not come to us now?

The Traveler

you walked past the colossal
gate with barred windows these

days adorned to say no praying,
kneeling, worshiping, spitting or

eulogizing allowed. emaciated
with travel, words scattered along

the way sparkled with your tale
of heading to a land full of those

who daily rouse to applaud the end
of senseless days that suffocate life.

you carried small bags with all your
possessions in them, firm memories

wrapped for the trip in scraps of paper,
family photos for trying times, even a

note from the village priest. more
than once you paused along the way

hiding from the moon to catch your
breath in the dark, eyes filling with tears

for those left behind in ruined places.
faintly, you laughed about the coming

change at the border's edge, and heaven
on wings you dreamed would meet you.

The Bell

ring the bells a little longer
for the fading year with the

carols that sweetly play of
peace on earth. with this

forgotten sound let all nations
ring uplifting cries against

the crime of war, the faithless
times, the hearts turned away

from your coming crown
of thorns. ring the bells for the

spilled blood where God lives,
for the clamoring throng beneath

the light of the spirit fed Star, for
the helpless of sight, the broken

mouths, the bloodied heads, wrinkled
laborers hands, and beggars cold tonight.

ring the bells above the graves, in
darkened homes, and hardened hearts,

yes, ring the bells, let them witness
Christ in mercy has come.

The Visit

I walked the block today
past the corner barbershop

with speakers over the front
door that played the music

of our world and made
walkers stand quietly to

ponder thickly the past
year like it was another

time. wandering in dreams
was the stained-glass window

on the big church familiar
to the mothers who work

like servants downtown
from five to nine each

day for little kids who should
not spend a lifetime on these

streets. I walked past the
coughing windows with the

shades pulled up, inside the
people filled with love's highest

longing, pitched broken English
to others on the sidewalk who

planned to spend the night chasing
hope to all the corners for the

sake of the bitter, the shivering, the
wretched, and overlooked poor.

Wait

on the corner I have a friend
who every day is troubled

by the silent birds with long
tails flicking on lamp posts

denying they are creatures of
sound. I thought his heart

would break waiting for them
to release a sweet song to help

him shatter all the time
he spends turning in circles

beneath city windows that
never open. the unknown

that swallows so many
yearly is always in front

of him but he tauntingly
waits for a sweet dream

to resist the morose world of
the walking dead. now and again,

he will stand on the corner
kneading bread with a big

smile that announces a perfect
hope is to him nearer, still.

The Well

by the ancestral well tucked
in the forest deep, that place

where the innocent were slain,
history shuffles toward truth.

birds above our heads today
sit on the wild branches of old,

speaking of the earliest cultures
now gone that we come to weep.

this well taught us how to live,
sing, dance, and mourn. With every

drink it gave the earth, the sky,
the sun, the moon became the sacred

world to us. Here awake this
night, we eat and drink beside it,

still.

Robin Williams

here lies another funnyman
in darkness making our hearts

skip knots. so many have
made meaning of life with you

filling their lines with laughter
never finished by any added

verse, but today we weep
memories that drown our hearts

thinking of you pale dead in
the lonely grave. we understand

little of death's arrival, how it
dressed to meet you, why it came

with wordless shouting, or silently
knocking at your door. we will try

not to speak of sadness when the
wintering birds return soon to darken

the skies, gently bidding us to the
stillness of your passing. and, in fearful

journeys, swinging us toward darkness,
we shall do our best to see you still

giving us the gift of magnificent delight.

The Prayer

Lord, I pray this ordinary moment
reaches up to you and talks as I do
about these streets that know how

longing is really a heaven day with
no screams, or weeping, or freezing
hearts, or agonizing dread to steer

us away from your gaze. I hold
my head in my hand waiting now
for your warming Sun to cast its

yellow light across the avenue
that smells of peeled oranges and
talks to us beneath a singing sky

with birds in flight you made. Lord,
save us in your memory like water
in your hand that never spills, include

all the simple corners that make us
us happy, the hot whispers in the
failing light that seek your open arms

always. Lord, on this ordinary day
take time to listen to those the world
will never grace with monuments, lean

closer to their tender and patient minds,
their stumbling steps, their wearied days,
and hear when they choking ask: how

long?

Undocumented

a dream hurried us here
from all the villages where

stones speak of massacres and
faith is consumed each day by

death. we have come to the land
of our dead who live in the smiles

of the river, the sandy desserts,
the starry night, and the voices of

so many who perished in your prisons.
we have come with truth to place in

front of those who murder history
in the papers with pitiable deluded texts.

we lug across the border stories of
the carefully omitted filth your public

never reads. we cross your fictive gate
hoping for a kinder world with people

who will not hesitate to stand against
sin, nor hold the hand of the bleeding God

who led our way. we come saying
you will not find a better prayer

than the tired look on our face.

Suspects

I woke up this
morning feeling
sick about America

and picked up the
telephone to call
the equal opportunity

office in the nation's
capital responsible
for making us invisible

to her gaze. America
why no memory carved
in time from listening to our

hoarse voices saying we
too live among the victories,
the sorrows, the mountains and

valleys, the waking cities, and
sleepy camps. endlessly America
you march confused into the dark

woods leaving us to cook, clean,
wash and care for your children.
why do you suspect us at home,

keep watch on the corners, along the
border, and with all purity of prejudice
keep this land unfree. America look

deeply at the ancient days, how they
beat with seasons borrowed from
alien lands, and you will conjure up a

different tune with trumpets
made from our countless bones.

The Fall

I sit in a city café listening
to news of hope ended by

the followers of darkened
religion who dance above

victims' graves. the silence
of midnight is scorched with

the terrified faces of the murdered
who vainly pleaded mercy from

the friends of a psychopathic God.
with the innocent bleeding, all those

to whom evil is done, we lean down
with shattered hearts and knell beside

the shot to denounce such boastful
visions of hate. I sit listening to

torturers gleeful shouts trying to detect in
the silent spaces what burial God is now

preparing for them. I sit in a city café
pale before the great puddles of blood

spilled in the name of promises that
will never be kept by the skittish

leaders who dare take the name of
the most High into dungeons of

punishment and death. I sit in
this café begging for them to confess

there is no room in heaven for the
barbarous who make a mockery of

peace shedding innocent blood. Yes,
your day will come . . . .

Till Later

we never counted time
talking into the dim night

wondering how life moves
forward with so little to

interrupt the sadness. now
that you have departed

to the world of sacred ash
death does not even dare

threaten us with shadowy
silence. we see darkness join

the everlasting procession
toward a distant light that

greets our deepest questions
with the simple thought that

divinity lives most assuredly
with you, now. we imagine

you peer into this world that
longs to find God's promises

and our gates of prayer swing
wide open for you to sweetly

walk into our smiling hearts.

Get out!

when shall we listen to the
voice that struggles to be heard,

the homeless kid that requires a
place, or see the dreadful waste

the callous dare to call a life.
in this dark where all our ghosts

slowly drag home, stalking all the
places of the heart that make our love

afraid, when shall we see the tenements
with a thousand rooms welcome the

unaccompanied child desperate for
just one. they play, they laugh, they

cry in coffins of detention far from
mothers' arms in a country mad with

hate for kids who raise brown hands
up to heaven in desperate cries for help.

how long shall they be seen as less
than vulnerable human beings, a peril

to national life, a deformity of God's
creation on whom the door must shut.

when shall we stand up to such unreasonable
fear for which even God has no words? When

shall we dream of peace, good will, and
precious life together with these homeless

young?

The Distance

it was winter, evening
shook beneath the glitter

of distant stars, and the streets
were paced by people who counted

the passing years piteously
waiting for heaven and earth

to change places. some hurried
past the corner with unexplained

lapses of memory that once
questioned what have we done to

anger God? an old man, his hair
moving in the cold wind, gazes into

the distance, each step on the
crusty sidewalk he measures with

a heart beating with enthusiasm
from another time, then he reaches

the faint light of a street lamp-post
thinking of all the dreams that

have grown older than his years.

The Rosary

walking the avenue this
evening the smell of peeled

oranges on the old
man's disguised cart

fills the air, and the sweet
scent halts the city gloom.

old women who cling
to every breath, pray on

on the sidewalk with rosary
beads in hand, and a snoopy

little brown boy stops in wordless
stare, until his mother pulls him to

the next corner. they quickly cross
to the far more mysterious world

of a street where the air is
always sweet, and the people

who live on it look to heaven
certain of a more precious future

still to come.

The Church

moments alone
sitting in a pew
behind an altar of

wood in a church
white folks left
us after savage

summers waiting
for some God to
lead us to life.

thinking of the
people listening
for the sweet

words that will
prompt them from
the shadows to

their feet gripping
street signs with
the Word you send

to carry them beyond
each daily prison
to the promised land.

Mount Pleasant

we gathered in
an ex-European
church to deal

up memories that
travel behind rough
faces on roads with

a power to charm
hard times. we
assembled to hear

voices long muted
by the architects
of lies, to listen

to songs with something
for those who can not
even hear God speak.

we came to the little
ex-European church
open to the hoarse

voices of a people
evangelized by the
gallows telling it

the way it is
to keep us from
never knowing.

Stop

I sent for you
because the thousand
excuses you make on

the other side of
the town keep the
infant twins in the

Rivera apartment you
never visit in front
of a television set

dying of AIDS while
Mister Rogers sings
it's a beautiful day

in the neighborhood.
I sent for the police
Chief who wants to lock

up their junkie parents,
the politicians who want
votes, the "putas" who

walk your side of the
street with married men
who want to be pleased,

the religious leaders who
pray for you to overlook
the questions junkies, whores

and dying kids ask. I sent
for you all because so
much talk of changing the

world on your side
of this town is cheap
now and at the hour

of our certain death.

Praise

in the barrio we
we long to breathe
God's grace on the

corner where Tito
shot his young uncle
following an argument

about a job lost at the
local A&P supermarket.
we long to dry tears

in the light that keeps
us from being trampled
under and offers strength

to count the years. in
the barrio, we seek that
heaven where there is no

dying a little each
day. but today with
the blood stains fresh

beneath our feet only
images of the people
who eat their fill while

promising better days
to come, arise. so we gather
to pray to God once again not

to let more lives be crushed
nor a single child fall in the
next hour. . . we beg a listen!

Voices

I saw maids in the park
wearing second hand

shoes talking beneath a
tall tree with birds on the

branches in song. I
heard them say they

stopped looking for
answers to the questions

God's promises long
ago stirred. their memories

of home like a tired
companion never makes

our blindness see. the wind
tossed dirt and the oldest

women on the park bench
began to weep for all the

dead buried in her heart.

The Playground

pretty soon
they will ask about
the boys living on the

street who come by the
little playground in
the afternoon. they will

guess the kids names and
how many of them will be
dead by the year's end. they

will not hear the children talking
of older brothers locked in
jail, while jumping on monkey

bars above a chipped wood
surface that breaks falls. they
will not mention how these

kids are waylaid daily by death
in a world that delivers little
hope from God. soon they will

ask which of the kids wrote
on the corner wall "Bro,
who gives a shit about us."

The Ride

on the subway one
morning while tossing

words to heaven
it came to me that

God is a good friend
of the poor in a world

that warns you not
to ask for justice.

then I looked at one
end of the rail car

and saw the man with
the sax who played

with a sign dangling
from his neck that said

in big letters "please
give for my daily bread."

a women next to me
opened her run down

bag for loose change
reliving momentarily a

dream of life without
damn chains. her dry

coughs then broke the
silence the rest of the ride

downtown.

God Has Pity

I walked down the street
believing God has pity

on all the ten year old
boys this night sitting on

the last steps of the apartment
building cooking dope to draw

into small glass eye-droppers
with needles at the end.

I stopped on our corner sure
of God's pity for the strung-out

kid snatched by an overdose
who left us only a parting sigh.

I woke up this morning certain
God must have less pity on

all these churches in the
neighborhood full of

prayer and godly people
who never do enough.

Been Waiting

Rudy's waiting on the corner for his
big hit. he's been waiting now for ten years
and the tracks in his arms
where Senora Heroina does come quiets

him for the wait while promising a
more complete destiny someday. he's
been waiting for the lover he
dreams of, for bitterness to run away,

for a blade of grass to grow from the
crack in the sidewalk that he stares
at in the wait, for Orchard Beach

to be in his pocket so he can reach in
for a calm feel to living; he's been waiting
for the welfare check, for the roaches to
take a walk from his one room where there

ain't no food no way. he's been waiting to
kick a jones he doesn't have, for his mother
who long ago said good-bye, for his country to

be born in him. he's been waiting for Lelo, who
left the waiting corner to join the navy and kick
his brothers' asses down in Vieques under orders

just to live. he's been waiting for spring and summer
and fall and forget about winter because
the corner is cold. he's been waiting for the

right time of day or night to think about
waiting some more.

Home Street

broken glass, bottle caps, asphalt blacktop commune
as silent streets in repressed violence remain
victims of loneliness.
ebony-skinned and curly-haired a Latino boy stands
by 1203, his stoop, eating sugarcane.

a corner knows the passage of time if not of us.
it mirrors death, soaks up murderous blood. knives
leave sheaths and enter bodies as machetes
fell cane. bodies drop, spilling blood,
another infamous story of the block.

city morgues fill with emptied hearts,
a corner speaks of such in silence.

days without yester...like motherless boys
half-lit blocks survive, disdained shamed
half burnt out and yet the pigeons fly by
unburdened, careless, like a Latino dream.

"Pee Wee, you're dead!" was it the corner took
your life, the prison of your kind? or the knife?
were you so emptied? your Latino ebony is gone
white ice, the corner your memoriam.

empty streets empty feeling, if such can be barren
in their reach stretching to arrive,
lost inside of searching's places.

Violence

now light the candles to
find your way on streets
where children run for

cover when they hear
guns shout past them
and cry for it all to

stop. bring the candles
and gather around the coffin
of the twelve-year old boy

death stepped toward in
a war ignored by those
who draw deep breaths

in places never darkened
by violence and fear.
above his grave for too

many others all roads
lead to the same silent
ground where family and

friends stand beneath
a tent of stars with fierce
grief and pain that will not

ever end.

The Corner

remember the corner where
Rudy stood day after day waiting
for something good to happen,

always dispensing advice to the hurt,
and giving names to stray dogs roaming
the block in search of food beneath

the shattered bricks and wood of
fallen tenements. do you recall
the Laundromat where he would

wrap himself away from cold
winter winds, share a bottle of wine
with junkies too stoned to think their

names. how about the time Rudy talked
about burning tears pouring down
his face one cold night, while buried

beneath rags collected from garbage
bags and church storage bins. Rudy waited,
and waited, and waited for the Angels to

come on that corner but like a dessert
mirage in the bright sun of an arid day
they never bothered to show up.

14th Street

an exhausted Saturday afternoon
holds in its fleeing arms latino
smiles themselves first shaped on

islands in the ocean and villages
in Central America. from all across
the city they have gathered in this

market place where a listening ear
can hear latino nations speak through
the memory of refugees and the independence

dreams of Boricuas. they gather
to cradle each other in history for a few
moments and drive away their invisibility

in America. stories are shared about
when the land in El Salvador will grow
food for the people instead of export, of

undocumented Nefatali who made his way
to New York from the Dominican Republic
arrested last week in a factory raid,

of the pregnant junkie mother Leonor
who gave birth to twins infected with
AIDS, and the little Methodist church in the

barrio with closed doors all week. beside
a merchandise bin two women speak of how
the children are having difficulty at school,

roam the streets, and are left alone. they
remind each other how that was the road
which led Hector into a grave at age 10

14th Street

from a drug overdose. here the world of
latino struggle encounters a language
of hope deeply carved in the hearts of

exiles from another land and those who
are born strangers in this place called

the United States of America. . . . .

Children

the laughter of children
is like tiny stones dropped

in a deep well when all
else sleeps the hours

of night away for a
new and sublime day.

their games are like
butterflies in a field

of flowers moving from
one paradise to another

celebrating eternity
amused. when life

embarks to sadness
hear them romp in

full smiles the length
of time. . .

Homeless

it's cold for sleep in
the park tonight and

no one is around to
talk life back to

warmth with memories
of days long left in

a world never scared
by snow. the block

pigeons are quietly
resting with a few

keeping watch for
all the rest who

prefer to miss the
common grave that

prankster children
would with joy

prepare for them.
the buses, like

nightly medicine, role
by taking their light

beyond the park,
where homeless

guests with tightly knotted
hearts look on wondering

which way is home.

The Lord's Prayer

Our Father in a heaven of
better days Lela shouts
your name daily from the

corner where she preaches
from a Bible with all manner
of reports about you to a

people who tell the sadness
of death, illegal work, hunger,
jail, and lack. they gather

every morning to listen
to some finished feature
that will help make your

kingdom come, and place
your residence in heaven
into their daily strife.

with worn goodness they
pray for daily bread on earth,
moan for life without debt,

and cry about the impossible,
ahead. abuelas wearing crosses
around wrinkled necks, rub their

calloused hands, praying for
better days, rescue from evil,
and this world a meeting place of

friends.

Black Out

when the lights went out
in the city people shouted
from the windows the world

is ending, at last! no more
penny wages, mopping floors,
cleaning toilets, washing

dishes, short-order cooking,
busing tables, babysitting,
dumping trash, or taking

it from bosses. when the
store alarms went off and
people ran with bundles

in the dark, they thought
God had finally come,
and all the candles bought

that year in la bodega
made sense. but the kids
alone in the apartments

betrayed such wild claims
stumbling in the dark for
candles to read the watches

that told them when mothers
would come home from
work to put things right.

the next morning
they would go to school
just the same and see

the same old gum-shoe color
guard holding a flag some
say only speaks English.

Piece Work

God knows where all
the fake jewelry went
that our young Puerto Rican

mothers assembled sitting
around the kitchen table
talking of old dreams and

memories of the island. They
all believed in miracles
and never forgot to pray in

Spanish so all heaven
above the streets of the
South Bronx could hear.

Ana's swollen stomach moved
then with a life inside
already well-fed by love

in a world of little bread.
in the other room children
laughed at television shows

featuring people who looked
different and happily wrestled
away the very time which one

day would hand them to
afflictions too great for
debating truth with God.

one cloudy night a mother
died after a long illness
a piece of costume jewelry

shaped like an angel was
placed on her burial dress
for the final long good-bye.

the kitchen table-talk was
not the same nor the other
room so noisy . . . . . .

Once

once we played on
streets the ordinary
games that amused

elders on the block
with laughter until
night fell. evenings

we sat on the curve
looking up at telephone
lines where old sneakers

swung on thin wire by
their different colored
laces in a naive heaven

made for those looking
for the dullest answers.
them days the radio station

played our favorite salsa
tunes making hanging
out an occasion where

friends passed dance
steps from nameless
stoops to the whole city.

yes, we hardly ever slept,
and never believed God
made us for dead-end streets.

Fire

the local priests did not call
on people in the building set
aflame by an angry father

who abandoned his sober God
when he found his daughter living
with a pimp and shooting dope

to soothe a tortured self. the
angels did not sing when he
walked by the apartment of the

porter who made just enough for
hunger, cigarettes and sobbing. the
arsonist carried his ache past

resting pigeons on the roof,
nervous like vermin keeping
out of sight, climbed down the

fire escape, broke a window and
fell into his daughter's place deader
than when the journey faintly echoing

stop, began. the trump of Jericho he
sounded came from gas poured on a
bed set ablaze in whose white flames

the dead testified loudly of his wicked
shame. there was crying in the street,
while the building exhaled its flames, and

disaster towed our homes away. still, no
priest ever came, no praying, no eulogizing,
no talking, no kind face, no useful word from

all so-called decent folk. the arsonist just slipped
into silence, and the people filled their goblets
with tears for sweet homes turned to ash.

The Witness

I've come back to the
city weeping old tears
provoked by the shattered

lives miracles ignore.
I see churches that
did not flee the horror

of this ghetto still
conjuring hope for all
the people who yearn for

a God who does not shorten
days nor answer prayers
with a colossal silence.

I walked past the finest
business on the block
where abuelita was laid

in a coffin made of
the lightest wood
our money could buy

aware of her last words
warning against every life
in the neighborhood becoming

a grave. then, I paused before
the mural painted on the wall
of a building at the end of

the street to read the names
of friends now dead to this
ghastly side of the South Bronx.

Jesse

I held you against
my chest years ago when
hope dared not forsake

our days. you slept
for hours making me a
pupil of a new world

unfolding. I will never
forget the grand smile
that rushed across your

face that first time you
rode a bicycle thinking of
flight while I ran behind

you keeping balance. yes
every pine wood derby race
was lost by our silly looking car

shaped entirely by love and
my unskilled hands yet you
managed to strain a look

toward the finish line each
event no more lacking in
hope for a full victory.

son, one night soon will
give you a feeling untouched
by any storm that a father's

love will never end.

Stumble

we stumbled one morning
on your body beneath a stairwell

in a Faile Street building.
you had on your Army issued

shoes, dingy white tee shirt, old jeans
and a crucifix the St. John's Church

priest gave you. the military police
came the night before looking to

take you back to base for a swift
dispatch to the killing fields

of Viet Nam. no one gave you
up to the MPs who regularly visited

the block. I wanted to tell your
mother got a barber's license, opened

a little beauty salon just up the street
from where you lay so dead. your brother

still invites us over to play Monopoly
with him behind the same stairwell, he

sometimes brings flowers to the spot
and together with painful doubts about

God above we bless your sweet name,
Manny.

Snowy Day

snow covered sidewalks
make the lame old-man think

of the Boricua flag on an old
wood pole outside his apartment

window. on streets singing and
bleeding, this old man has carried

hope expecting to awaken in some
lost paradise. at night he writes

in the soiled pages of a red
spiral binder of the people

who no longer speak to each
other despite pleas for a little

time. he left the big church
where others babbled of things

never seen and talked stories
of Jesus who kept them enslaved.

walking into the bodega on
the corner he looked for answers
in all the aisles. one day, he

told me laughter falling from
his lips we will stop burying the
dead who came to this country

with dreams that only turned into
brooms.

The Anniversary

the first day beneath an
infinite sky, the crowds

walking the sidewalks in
apparent cheer, you loosed

a wondrous tale the wind
carried past time lurking

in the shadows to me. I held
you in my heart where sadness

now stunned plunged me ever
deeper into love. the Fall leaves

rustled above your head, while
birds danced on branches for

what seemed the full evening.
then, my heart pounding with

sublime bliss completely shouted
from the rooftops I love you, now

ever more and longer than the last
starry lights above shall live.

The Crucified

you never talk of the
barrio where the word
of the poor rages against

a world secure in wealth.
you never think of the
crucified nailed in the slums

by bullets to a wood that
mocks our simple deeds
and frail faith in tomorrow.

you were not there to see
the blood-stained corner
made by a four year old girl

who received the bitter
end of a shoot-out between
fifteen-year old boys over

an indolent stare. in summer,
you didn't walk into the smoke
of trash fires burning in empty

lots filled with a pity inhabited
by those who die before their
time without tribute, or reply.

how dare you speak of Truth
in the cathedral not knowing
how faces fall to sadness, or

showing light that leads to
sorrow for those who mourn,
alone. someday, when you see

but dimly on one of these streets,
truth will meet you in the scarred
flesh of Christ said present in

the poor.

Shot

she walks the streets
with memories swallowing

the graffiti walls, junkies, lost
dogs, and fierce wounds past

the building with an old man
who repairs watches that never

tell the right time. with startled
eyes she spots people at the bus

stop, including a young girl,
who is silent. on this block of

earthly paradise unknown, why
she wonders can't we find each

other in good times. evenings,
after making all the corner

rounds chanting songs of
heavenly fellowship for

the noisy streets that keep
us quietly weeping, she

stops to glance at the saddest
avenue around, where in an empty

space her son cried a last
good-bye, with an immeasurable

look in his eyes pleading for a
little more life. she walks on and

in her bitter well we drown.

The Crossing

we feel time passing
like an express train

on a cold day in an empty
station water dripping

from melting snow
through cracks in the

overhead sidewalk. a chilly
breeze blows by our ears

coughing memories
into life from spaces

unseen. on this chilly
day the train will carry

us back to life in a
South Bronx project

where the management
cannot ever hear us

holler help sweet God. downtown,
jobs hang us each day on splintered

Crosses, while those in power
sit quietly unstirred by our howling,

and weeping and gnashing of
teeth at the miracles that never

come in this monstrous hell,
where wounds never close.

Brother

On Easter Sunday when my brother
died, the clocks ticked still in all the
bodegas, the pigeons circling above

him moaned, and a rainy night
was summoned into silence. I
alone saw how death arrived for

you like a needle in search of
thread, dressed no doubt with
darkness for the occasion, pleased

to drag you to a cemetery full of
bones. I screamed across the bridges
guiding me to you, passed all the

lonely church doors, the empty
windows, the fatherless boys, the
buses halting at the corner stop, to

find you in that night that never
passes, where you will now sleep
on. when I saw you at the morgue,

stranded like ever without a mother's
bosom or father's heart to shed a tear
for you, I was never more convinced

you were Good Friday's child.

Lela

in the morning,
while walking toward
the corner, I saw Lela

returning from *la misa,*
checking her watch in the
wind that pushed two doves

above her head. she heard talk
of ashes, dust and universal
love working said the priest in

the sadness of a violent age,
she listened to talk of the good
Lord in the world of the shamed

who gasp daily for air. you could
see truth seeping from her eyes
unto those who had once been

tortured and abandoned for dead
who sat quietly now on their Bronx
tenement steps. they smiled when Lela

walked by each Sunday always
whispering never leave your lot
simply to God. furious with infinite
love this woman made darkness

tumble in a tender light that
managed to settle in our hearts.

The Marina

he was found by
the docks pouring
the sadness from

his grieving heart
into waves gently
breaking the shore,

yet peace would not
come. he turned away
from the passing crowd

with poison tears
pouring down his
cheeks each one a

story of the magnificent
life, now gone. As if,
in the presence of God,

he raised stretched
arms in a strong wind
blowing off the sea,

but still no voice came
near. I shut my eyes when

he cried God above come,
come to sweetly listen.

Family

when I close my eyes
and see their faces in
the dark, life wakes

up jumping rope as if
tomorrow were stranded
in the distance. I held them
each in my arms imagining

the winding years, in warmer
love calling me beyond the
ruined shacks, to the simple truth

of beginning. what sweet
love each kid holds, so far
from the flimsy days of

threat, and closer still to open
arms. today, with a mind
of dreams in cold of winter,

all the bare places in surprise
splendor, with eyes closed,
full of the same faces, I smile

into the unknown.

The Stoop

this block was a
place to hang on

stoops until the first
light of the sleeping

city pushed us off the
low rent steps. nights,

the radio played symphony
Sid's show until daybreak,

and the questions cutting us often
in two stood alone. at midnight,

stories dropped of fishing on the
docks where poor city kids like

us bursting wildly inside dreamed
of a sail to sea, or the coco vendor

selling sweets to transit riders
headed to la playa de Orchard Beach.

until dawn, we shared stories like
the day that poured laughter over

the heart of the block, when water
sprayed from the pump cooling us

dropped old Chinos draws all the
way down to the blacktop street.

tonight, with fewer sitting on the
stoop a question is raised: who

declared the end?

Hope

when the star in the sky hangs
high above this long walk past

the dusty flowers, the odious gates,
the howling of other hate, and all

unforgiving fate, with breaking ease
we will sing the hope you whispered

in our veins that shouts there is time
to change. when the sorrowing of all

inhuman provinces steered through history
by Herod's shameless men comes to end,

the ghosts in the spotted mirrors who moan
of senseless war heard, the broken healed, the

hungry feed, the naked clothed, the imprisoned
freed, the stranger welcomed, the nation reborn

with hearts pounding out the peace
that makes our swords mere plowshares,

when we carry your hope to the miserable,
the lonely, the helpless, the guilty, the

dying that make so many run the other way,
when we plunge into deep darkness stumbling

to find the magnificent hope of your manger;
then, with certain cheer we shall see Christmas

here and forever near.

Lost Paradise

In the beginning
your God created
the barrios and slums

with words not found in
scripture that you use
for Sunday morning praise in

a church keeping distance
from the pain that makes
us human. you trample

life each time you sing and
pray to a God who does not
bother to show gracious love

to the poor living in a world
of crack, heroin, degradation,
genocide and death. in prayer,

you never mention the people
who cry for children locked in
prison or buried deep in potter's

field graves. though you sit
in a sanctuary lighted, holding
a Bible in fine dress, you refuse

to see the crucified One scaling
colossal mountains of grief.

The River

the day you crossed
the river God did not
deliver you from the

people blaming strangers
for the dark previously come.
you crossed the border on

a pale dawn day filled with
a dream that made you shudder
each step on the other stony bank

recalling the smoldering villages,
the blood-stained rivers, the veiled
cries, the savagery fled. lurking in

ambush loathing voices spewed
this is not the promised land for you,
nor the protected space to speak against

torture, violence, blasphemy and the
streets carefully finished gallows. you
swallow bitter tears when they shout

illegal to push you back across the
border to a land of boundless nightmares
paid for least we handily forget by the

blessed American dollar.

The Birthday

children bloat the house
with laughter on your
fifth birthday this

chilly November day. joy
crosses your face put there
by family and friends who make

memories with you to mark
birth once again. mother never
forgets to make all things

in love and your aunt Pat
whose years have run faster
than your own is present to

embrace the space you occupy
in all these hearts. you a gem
the earth has yet to know, my

little girl named Claire. you
are sweetness in the Soul, a
complete world of glee in a five

year old frame.

Sign of the Dove

at the Sign of the Dove
upper east siders sit at

small tables dressed for
jazz. a woman robed

in black lace surveys the
room with flashlight eyes

inviting notice. the female
vocalist sings a haunting

melody of sweetest care that
drives all the bitterness at the

end of a long winter's day far
away. people pouring into

the space rehearse by the bar
words for accidental meetings with

strangers who will saunter home
with breaking day, nameless.

the piano at the far corner of the room
is never silent, and sitting in front of it

a couple set ablaze with love brilliantly
stirring perform their way for anyone

who cares for deeper secrets to see.

Alone

in a cheap apartment
with paper thin walls
never like a home you sat

exhausted by the laughter
next door of an old lady
visited by friends. the

days when you kids shouted
mami have passed, leaving you
with trifling signs of life in

memories unable to push
aside the unforgiving images
of the kids your arms discarded.

what will they say of your
bony remains now in passage
to eternity? what did these kids

shout to the world on that good-bye
day? did they sob at your grave?
sweet mother God grant you peace
and the forgiveness no one dared

speak the day you passed away . . . . .

Delivered

today,
rain pours on the dusty
lots where the buildings stood

housing something deeper than
sadness. the sound of children

no longer playing, the old man
who used rum for a walking stick,

the little girl who fell to her knees
to argue with God, the grandmothers

who always sat at their windows
collecting neighborhood gossip, gone.

today,
the sound of dogs barking in
the distance tells us this place

has no need for religion.

Evening

listen to the evening song
fall on the failing light of

day in which there was nothing
but work to be done. it subdues

bodies dancing round each other
in the cosmic space of amorous

play. it rummages in bedrooms
for heart aches to cradle back to

more precious life. Listen
to this night chanting like a

sax on an empty street that
orders the quiet, the still, all

sadness to sleep. it pines like
a blue harmonica tune unworried

by the demented tales of an angry
world, unravelling the wild knots,

and with all incarnate value, rests in
the place of all the hurting to send

us into paradise sleep. listen to
the evening song yield gracious

mirth in all those places you sighed,
and tonight breath with me the lunacy

of love.

Washed Away

remember the corner where
Rudy washed outside in darkness
day after day waiting for some

magical gate to unlock a finer truth
than the wine that poured purely down his
throat, and the needle he kept deep inside a

vein. remember how he dispensed advice to
all the wounded on the block glistening blood
like Christ on the Cross. remember the alley

beside the Laundromat where Rudy nightly
smothered dreams wrapped in sacks to face
the bugle called winter that massed around

his feet forecasting a bitter end. battered by
the sound of his own groaning that no one
ever seemed to hear, he found time to share

cheap wine with people who lived too stoned to think
their names. remember that sleepless night in the filthy
tenement when he cried about his mother's silence,

the vain longing to know a father, and all the love
lost to him. I remember holding you in my arms,
grieving with you my way, and consumed by

tears declaring sweet brother in this hellish paradise
we are the world of love. then, despite a hatched plan,
in April Easter dark, death smashed down his paper door

screaming from afar nothing is ultimate, you see.
I wanted to tell you about taking that call in the poor
light of night I screamed at the God who shortened
your days. I wanted to say one day in the full

fragrance of heaven we shall met, again.

Halloween

we gathered in front of blue eyed
Victor's building moving about
the stoop looking at an old lady

leaving the bodega chewing on a
hunk of *day of the dead bread*. Grinning,
she licked the dusty sugar from her

finer than truth fingers. The weeping
women on the block with darkness
deep inside came back from Mass

dreaming they saw loved ones alive
in a heavenly mansion with a thousand
doors. Victor will soon come out in a

ragged gray sweater his Dutch mother
found in the Catholic thrift shop to
make him a hobo clown before leaving

for the night shift where the dead she
recalls will scream in the back of her throat.
Her son will spend the night knocking on

the apartment doors of people who remember
every speck of blood marking trails back to
places long ago fled. Halloween delirious with

trick or treat amusement is nonetheless
simple for the kids who take complete
brightness onto the scary streets.

Protest

justice has no bandaged eyes
on the streets bidding law
to her knees in the name

of an innocent child dead.
sorrow paced for weeks,
each night without full

sleep, while a jury busy
with calculations found a
way to favor a common

terror when it decided no
monstrous crime by the police
was done. the weeping can

now be seen in the faces of those
who march with muffled drums
asking that abysmal day to stop

long enough to hear the mourners
protective shouts for this beloved
Black son. pour away the festering

blindness, the victim blaming lies, the
hatred speech, the calloused hearts
dreaming their nightmares for us.in the

protest, march beyond the painful
sobbing and with our martyred King
bellow from the sidewalks and on

traffic ridden streets, "Let justice roll
down like waters" so no more
kids come to such a terrifying end.

Awake

some place near to here,
after the long night we

stood weeping beside the
graves of children, asking

what God will resurrect them
from their untimely deaths, choked

by their incredible silence, we see
their images carried down the street

to the church step. inside, we find
babies crying, children hungry,

broken hearted mothers in march
to Christ's altar with pictures of their

expired kin. they plunder
further into darkness, and pray

to a God who they believe stands
in judgment of the failing courts

with magistrates who never
hear the thousands like them

living in a world of relentless
daily mourning.

Christmas

it was winter, the streets
were crusted with snow, frost
had settled on the apartment

windows, pigeons cold a
long time were quiet in their
niches. people with the same

joy walking the bottle strewn
streets with kinder faces waved
their hands to greet the old, the

meek, the poor and the young
who strolled to church with
seasonal merriment. the stars

were closer to us on these cold
nights making us think about
the old men at the bodega who

trembled when opening presents
they did not expect saying Angels
sang Christmas hymns to them

all day long in Spanish. children
hungry for days tailed mothers into
mass craving food, warm clothes, a

toy beneath their fake trees, and
somebody to tell them one day
you will feel at home, the crooked

walls keeping you out will crumble
and this new world will sweetly

call your full name.

The Light

the light can be seen the
length of the avenue, tonight.
the air filled with silence is

split by a drunkard's song that
hastily stops, and the sound of a
few pigeons flying high to

another watch gives us peace,
somehow. there are no words
to pretend to know the silence

standing for all things, no answers
given in the dark, no blinding light
to cease us on the twisted roads,

no greater miracle around us than
the simple cries of children playing
on the street, mothers longing for

heavenly days, people who never
harp of their deep wounds, and the
old who find thousands of ways to

invent new hope for us. the silence
allows the unspoken truth of all the
grieving widows on the block, of blind

Tito who sees more than the downtown
crowd and knows like a diviner what the
future holds for our common lot. in this

hush, the loved ones searched for
in nightly dreams rise from ash, touch
the dark and walk with us to the

end of perfect streets where the dark
leaks a magnificent light from which
all intolerable ruin cannot slip away.

The New Year

though you are gone
and the days pale since

that last breath on all
the corners your name

is whispered. you were never
safe from hostile days and

always nameless for those who
prayed, you sank each year into

deeper sadness vaguely glad to
see each fresh new year. you

carelessly move now in our
memories, freely like the Sparrows

in the sky, telling a story in
the shadows of the hearts of

those who knew you well. and
now, the corners here keep your

wisdom in a box with instructions
for us to open at the last tick of the

city clocks.

Wait

on the corner I have a friend
who every year is troubled

by silent birds with their long
tails flicking on lamp posts

denying they are creatures of
sound. I thought his heart

would break waiting for them
to unwind a sweet song to help

him shatter all the long-denied
voids and turning in circles

beneath city windows that
never open. the unknown

that swallows yearly so
many is always in front

of him but he dares wait
for life sweetly streamed

to resist the dark, the edgy,
the grumbling, and the ample

world of the walking dead.
on the corner he kneads

bread you see with a kind
of perfect hope that assures

us daybreak is surely near.

Spider's Web

in a melody only known
to her listening ear, she

sang to me about the care
so lovingly spun in a dim

barn for the sake of a rather
innocent pig. we imagined

together while flipping pages
the morning dew that gathered

in Charlotte's web in the
quiet dawn that named all

the wonder to be found
in ordinary life, a chatty

space, and the sweetest love
of friends. as the story unfolded

the dreamy voices in the barn
awash in the loveliest faith

believed in life. then, the
dust collecting on Charlotte's

expired frame made my
daughter one more child

sobbing why the tolling
bell, why. whispering, I

promised to light a straight
candle in this dark to chase

away the dreams of weeping
with the life the brilliant spider

said is all it was ever meant.

The Window

when the child sat beside
the slightly opened window
chanting of Spring the potted

flowers on all the pebbly sills
inched toward birth to offer
us incense for uncertain days.

when we saw her keeping distance
from the stars, we made our way
down the avenue where darting

sparrows above our heads announced
in flight nothing else is love. by the
little park, below the window, squirrels

ran silent across patchy grass
and fallen leaves on time that
lingered in the neighborhood since

the first infant cried. in our voices
we carried all the tangled stories of
distant shores that nightly became the

sleep songs painting our children's
dreams. yes, that child knows that
even the piteous day cannot withstand

the riotous joy of looking past the
shadows at human love, sublime.

City

city of shut doors, open
curtains, and failing light

you always smile when
the boys playing stick ball

call your name. in you kids
fly kites on rooftops that soar

above the fashionable lights
beneath them to places farther

away than the dreams God
made in paradise. city awake

at night with music booming
delight, where nothing slips

into silence, and languages
mingle in public with signs

of deeper love, you call
by name. city clenching

the hand of those in sadness,
you pour in the empty stations,

the burning hearts, and a barely
hoping world the ripe sweetness

of a new day. city from your
rank towers children will soon

press their lips to your ear to
whisper from midnight sleep

I dream . . . .I dream . . . I dream.

The Feast

Outside, on the street the rumors
of peace slip into a vanishing day

while the quivering lips of
grandmothers who wander about

the world tell us they have seen
the promised child, and filled their

needs with good. Outside, Angels sing
whenever they stroll past the

unlit church with talk of
heaven now unfastened for an

Easter feast that will quickly
fade from memory in the coming

new year. Outside, children frolic
in winter breezes laying in their way

the hope of lofty dreams at his
feet. Outside, a star led people say

God descended from his heavenly
place to be simply with us.

American Dreaming

there are rooms in the South Bronx
cold like the street winter with walls

crumbling with the language of wounds
spat by the massing poor inside them.

on the dawn stumbling block a new face
is worn by the American dream on the front

steps of our building where the young children
are no longer to be found cause they fill the

cemetery plots across town. in madness knives
extinguish life staining memories with the blood

of an American dreaming people curbed
by merciless ends. the graffiti wall in the

neighborhood recalls Joseph who met death
in violent convulsions on a dirty rooftop a needle

settled deep in his veins, and the wearied mothers
behind grayish walls who earn the wages of old beggars

under sacks are always out of the uptown crowds sight.
the other day on the pitiless street corner, there in

the dark, elderly women talked of the mother of
the little girl accidentally shot by a stray bullet meant

for another who went back to Puerto Rico with
her daughter's corpse imprinted on her heart to

consume her days henceforth with horror. peace
the old ladies say long ago walked away from this

block.

South Bronx Street

a stain on the corner keeps
spreading like oil on paper
not making distinctions when it

comes following blood let from
the human frame that bellows pain
into space to hang on dirty tenement

windows. the Pentecostal storefront
preachers say Jesus who knows a
thousand deaths in the South Bronx

each day will soon save us. sure, I saw
this crucified lord on Southern Boulevard
just last week getting stabbed by the

Pepsi-Cola brothers for dope. I found
him screaming in the hallway of a
building on Longfellow Avenue laid

out on the floor looking up at me
through Esther's face that was beaten
bloody by a husband angry about

getting laid off work and all the
mouths at home to feed. I saw him
in the alley sitting beside the old man

sobbing for all the churches in the
neighborhood never visited by the
stranger who promises to keep the

darkness from plundering our lives.

South Bronx Soldier

there is no flag beneath
a South Bronx cemetery just

silence. you see it written on
the faces of the family who

whisper beside the grave the
the needle took his life. there

is no warmth in the casket laid
in earth to separate the dead

from the rest of us, deserted.
the cemetery gate will be painted

again next year to adorn this
place but there is no flag for

this one who went to his last
sleep with a needle in a vein

blessed by a pale god who left
him among the nameless dead.

La bodega

a brown suit man wheels
a grocery cart to the corner

searching for rest in each foot-fall
that leads back to the cell of a home.

looking out the window he recollects
the ocean breeze wet with the sea moving

in all directions and the sandy shores
of youth spent on his Puerto Rican isle

of enchantment, Borinquen. now, far
away, he sits in a barely furnished

room waiting for salvation to come,
always listening to a concert of voices

stored in his favorite rum that is kept
beneath the kitchen sink. sometimes,

he'll watch evening rain turning
his head toward the Puerto Rican

flag hanging above the bed, gently
and honorably bow, then drop tears

collected through years of
yearning for his paradise to be

free.

Sweet Kiss

enfold me in the place where
in your hour of hours beauty is

named, and I like a secret Rose
in flowering Red shall whisper to your

ear from the darkness nothing was
lost to the night that tried in vain

to hide you from me. with my
whole body I touch you, I dream

our lives inseparable, to speak
this indomitable love without explanation.

relentless tenderness, nothing
but light, carry me inside you, never

look away from me, and remember
I love you more than the beginning

of things.

Clocks

I walked the bleeding corner
today looking for the faces of
so many killed by others who

hide despair behind guns. my
eyes roamed the neighborhood
from the curve and noticed the

clocks in the bodegas not
telling time for the dead nor
those who will descend into

hell for them. the old men
who still live in the barrio
stare with uneasy eyes at the

young guys on the corner who
they can't understand but
fear. shadows stay eternally

on our streets while in them
we ponder a deep place inside
us where something has already

died. madness covers half
the soul of this barrio that
is home to a forgotten people

of this city where life goes
on never looking the other
way . . . .

Burning

they burn black churches
again denying God through
a violence that only fools

all manner of humanity
in their hearts. from a fire
in a bush that never lost

its life God spoke to
Moses of freedom for
all humanity—enslaved.

from the ashes of black
churches achieved by the
terror of a racist America

God recites bold words of
overcoming. out of fires
of hate that crucify the

certain beauty of God's
own creation redemption
draws near to make each

day a celebrated mixture of
people who see no face in
hate nor live to see others

dead.

Everlasting

the gladdest thing when the hours
turn to stone, is the faint light in the

darkness revealing the unknown,
the scent of flowers blessing the

evening with calm, and the
blunt utterance of hope rising

from our deepest flesh from
places most alive. beneath your

unending mercy we look up at
the stars in evening strolls with

wordless awe asking what next
and laughing let it come. in the

warmth of leaning night you
most High find ways to step

out into space to greet us. before
existence fades, we certainly shall

humbly sing look around you that
is God, so let your throbbing heart

remain untroubled and in good,
and perfect cheer.

Yom Ha'Shoah

sometimes I go back to the
candy store on Broadway to
see the old man with numbers

on his forearm who tried explaining
how he was ripped from his mother's
arms beneath a moon lit sky and taken

to a place to weep, to starve, to see many
only find death at the end of the
tunnel, not light. he always whispered

of this hell he preferred to forget but
the disfigured faces begging for life
would always visit him in dreams and

even demand a hearing at the counter
where he served children like me scoops
of ice cream in a soda glass. after all

these years, I go back to sit with him
for hours wailing of the world turned
upside down, watching his face display

the wretched whose lives were shortened
settle for witness on his wounds. what I
would not give for a better world to give

this old man whose home remains now a
drifting cloud wrapped in night that will
not turn.

Unaccompanied Minors

one day you will walk out of
the darkening room among the

mothers whose children fled gangs,
bullets, and the unending stench of

death, to end in jails run by patriotic
pilfers. down the mountain passes,

the failing light, in cities engulfed
by northern winds, you might someday

see round faces with scared tears,
learn their names, and hear stories

of the innocent with no known address,
rejected. one day you will wash your

thoughts in the same cold water, wonder
about all the saviors taking pictures of those

who suffer in plain sight, and never
set them free. for once you may even

wipe the dust from that wonder book
that makes faithful old woman

cry to a merciful God they believe
will keep these children from perishing

on yet another suffocating rubbish
heap of history. the time will come

when you will sit for prayer in that quiet
room where you were never moved to love,

and meet complete silence.

Follow

come memory follow me to
the weeping corner where
every night the truth in the

church is put to shame, then
on Monday is placed on the
kindergarten chalkboard, for

kids who cannot write the alphabet
and know too well how to carry talk

of the dead. come memory see life
fumbling among the buried in places

along the street mothers told us
hold down the edge of dreams

and keep the world from hearing us,
the others. come memory listen to

my off key voice for a little while
longer about the boy who recognized

his brother in a lonely cemetery far
too dark for any to see his tears.

come memory see the faces
smiling in the distance for

mercy's sake begging time
for the kind of life much finer

than all the words declared
in Sunday morning worship.

Night

child, in a dream, cry
the wounds away, sleep,
sleep, the fear you thought

coming through the window,
to hold you speechless like
a corpse. in the morning

wake from sadness, sit
on the brick stoop of your
building, and never leave

the best days you even now
can summon.

Pocket Memory

as a child, he went to the
zoo one morning complaining

of a sky giving so much water
he never felt like smiling into

heaven's eyes. before birds
stirred for another day of

song and flight across the
gardens skillfully kept by the

employees of the department
of parks, he'd walk quickly

to the sweetest place that let
him see what seemed talking

trees, two seals drowning misery
in play, and his favorite elephant

nearing middle-age still preaching
salvation to the curious throng with

every careful flip of her trunk.
something happened to him

wandering those forest lanes
cleverly hiding animal words

that only he could breathe into
completion. on visits, he always

walked beyond what others could
see toward some light ahead.

After School

I know the picture, the boy
posed for that late Spring,

after a day of child's-play
hung on his head, while the

red-winged black birds sat
calling from the branches

of the patio tree. like a beggar
lined up for bread that morning

after all these years it is with me
still. a finer truth cannot be

found in all my books reaching
for the world wearing old grew

sweaters. the moment passing
that fine day like fog loosed from

the earth on the saddest lanes
mumbled beneath a luminous sky

life is only air, yet I who lived
so long where the shadows forever

linger proclaimed far from
the questioning reach of all

that leaves us with irreverent
dread faith in endless love.

Earth

what can be said now when
nearly everyone considers the

Gods are dead, and you exquisite
mother free for thousands of

years are thought just earth
more thoroughly owned.

how long shall we wait for
them to kneel before your

sun rising behind the hills
at dawn, the moon painting

the sky in silver, the rivers
emptying into the sea, birds

soaring the breaking clouds,
and all relations in every step

at peace. when will they
see your grassland hair, or

feel your brown embrace,
yielding this gift life you

give with mystery, no
gloomy taint, and years

forever turning.

Sight

to watch you walk across
the street carving space in

the city like a holy vision
without need for robed

figures, sacred rituals, or
pious relics, and with simple

steps communicate the memory
of heaven, made standing on the

Sunday corner this morning a pearly
time of travel to the One promised

better than in Speech. sometimes,
on an ordinary street where kingdoms

are not made we can see almost enough.

Unnoticed

the news does not rush
to cover us convulsing

beneath the policeman's
shoe, or shouting fiercely

from yet another pool of
blood. no big crowds are

stirred to march, and citizens
scarcely shake their heads,

when hearing of our last
and agonizing breath.

San Romero

in the chapel where you
were killed many years

ago the world became
familiar with its despair,

it saw at last the spread
ashes of the poor, and

witnessed darkness trying
to plunder life, but God's

Angels announced your
Word cannot be undone.

madness lifted its veil from
the long pageant of Sunday

strollers who now walk
past these grayish doors

into the infinite light you
placed in the way. still,

you said divinity does not
come in hushed prayers, but

with the blood of paradise
you too shed like Christ for us.

in your chilling altar death
remembered, hope rises in

us now with no end.

Freddie Gray

the news the sidewalk bears
makes us dissolve in tears

for the shattered body of yet
another young man for whom

no gate in heaven opened when
flattened by senseless cops'

blows. the violent pain makes
us tremble in this other war on

city streets the authorities with
heavy breath all too easily flee.

beyond what the law has eyes to
see those who march the streets

remind us of the terrible screams
stating with long processions into

darkest night nothing is fixed by
another body laid to rest beneath

a bloody field of lilies.

Gravestone

we dragged this giant stone
from the graveyard that is now

addressed to you with fragments
of hundreds of destroyed hearts

no longer eager to say amen. among
those longing for these funerals to

end too many now say God does not
have pity for so many kids laid in

the ground for imperfect rest, still
others hope the killer cops who put

them under will not find Divinity's
pity at all. we dragged this giant

stone passed every corner our dearly
departed knew believing they smiled

at us from the distance to place it
by the wall of the dead in a world

sunk with sin. look, do you hear the
mournful sounds of mothers who

became strangers to tenderness and
hope? Can you see the darkness

made of cold moving now in our
hearts?

Light

without applause we march
in the dark amid protest noise

loosened by heaven above seeking
justice below. in this nightmare

where the innocent stopped living,
we walk the streets carried by

a light inside that persuades us
with blessings of peace to find

in all this sorrow the pitched
light of a magnificently merciful

God. the evening vespers where
defiant prayers are loudly recited by

the faithful now in despair tell the
story of the city's fall that will never

figure dimly or curve out of sight.
when morning breaks we will still

cry with palms raised in the air beside
those who have seen death already

in black and brown faces wearing closed
eyes and names the police in their darkest

hour never knew. through it all we
bear witness even in our sorrow to

God crucified and with us.

Learning

if all you know of truth
now speaks loudly to those

who cannot understand the
curses of the poor the world

contains, then prefer to let
every Eden gate be opened,

let no life be crushed, and
injustice crumble with its

weight. if sacred wisdom is
something you have learned

with others who mourned the
Crucified One, then ask the

pallbearers jealous of his pledges
not to darken earth. if you walked

this far with the nets of doubt
withdrawn with every footfall

even smaller than any eye could
see, then hear those now who carry

what seems like a thousand years
of grief in their hearts, and do not

slip from them with silence.

The Pause

stop the clocks today long
enough to forget about the

years of light reduced, the
pictures turned to flames,

the sobbing eyes that ache
for home by rummaging the

self. do not dismiss from
view feathers whistling in

the wind in the tangled park
that transmit a sudden waking

breaking open, like two white
doves in the wilderness eagerly

watching.

Rain

listen to the old brown
faced man standing in the
rain imploring those who
travel the avenue in early
evening light to spare some
lullaby change. he has been
drinking rain for days while
watching for signals about
life for him a second time alright.
the burdened clouds keep pouring
on streets called home, while
with a troubled gaze he looks
to heaven for an open gate that
will keep him from dying a little
more tonight on the curved spaces
of the corner. remind everyone
of the way this old brown faced
man borrows hope clinging to
an enchanted dream of a kinder
future that inside of him already
peacefully beats.

The Saint (May 23, 2015)

today, you declared with lightning
shooting from your lips, in the world
the lords of terror huddle from
now in silence, a saint for us.
from the distance, the transparent news
makes the blind see the old gallows, the
aching wounds, and this blessed hope
recalled with tambourines shaking above
the thieving graves. as night embraces
the jubilant crowd carols, the divine mercy
that made death come to life in gentle
voice decrees in the name of riches no
more misery, ashes and death. today,
you spoke the name of a saint for our
time who assembled words that swirled
to heaven and gently settled within us.
today, we proclaim to those who yet
savage love your dark has already come,
so in forgiveness change.

The Bridge

listen,
suppose I take a long walk
in the falling night, lean over

the bridge railing shouting
for God to personally speak.

Listen,
suppose I set up a booth at the
other end with people bursting

with superhuman dreams and
longing to hear of the Coming

future that will make them sing
with feverish joy of long haired

angels tearing down dividing
walls and hearts turned to stone.

listen,
suppose I gossip from my soul
of God quietly watching what

we hunger to become and point
to the distant mountains beneath

the burning stars that will no
doubt be forwardly moved.

listen,
suppose I say in this crossing
inside of us no pit of ashes can

permanently beat.

Father's Day

into this world this child
came to greet us where

the shadows never linger
and joy peacefully embraces

us for the long walk ahead, where
we see the rich promises of love

awake. Look. heaven leaned
in our direction this night of

blazing stars to give us much
to say. Look. this Holy rush

of shining hope now with us
will pour out her dreams until

every truth is clear.

The Little Park

Children play in a dusty park
with dirty faces laughing a game

of tag round watchful grandmothers
familiar with the truth paraded by

their young. a few young dogs
join the chase barking gleefully

in all directions with tails keeping
time for a lazy afternoon of fun.

care makes a repeat appearance
in the game more times than the

youngest child can count and
no one forgets to look up to

heaven to share a warm smile.

Emanuel AME

dreams here are always good
even though it is not easy these

days to feel the sweet ground
beneath our feet. you see, the

earth is lit with the thousands
of lives that only spoke of hope

even in the harshest times, when
the wind bellowed with Vesey's

ruin, the majesty of secret routes,
the knowledge of Booker T. and

the celebrated freedom of King.
in the ache of wounds, our mighty

dreams unbent, in forgiveness yet
disclose the force that put us here,

together. yes, our dreams are enough
to overwhelm hateful men with frozen

souls who answer God above darkly
with dreadful acts that swallow innocent

lives, whole. yes, we shall overcome
the sadness, the fear, the anger, the crying

day with the good news that always and
everywhere breaks the killing chains.

Evening

I went out to the little park
where the first church bells

rang far away, and brown
trout swam in the stream, and

people stood on the banks praying
for nothing in particular. the day

faded the length of the walk,
magnifying beauty from the

branches of trees slipping
into silence now that the busy

blackbird is not cracking seeds.
those seen here circling the

narrow paths thinking what
happens when faces turn

to bone, pause in these
woods for a look at the better

hope talked up in the heat of the
bell ringing church last Sunday.

Morning

I sit beneath a tree, my
eyes closed to savor the
sweetest breeze, and the

dreams here are not too bad.
a bird above twitters a song that
stops my breathing long enough

to recollect the line: *I am with*
you always. in this moment
reaching out with prayer as the

sun comes up I say dear God
overhear these poor words
speaking now for all who sit

in the rising light unable to
rejoice, give them faith and
eyes with which to see the

hope that even lets your
butterflies swim, walk them
into the new day with a simple

will to live past their original dust
in the certainty and presence of
your most gracious saving love.

Get Out

once more, the church
gate's locked and inside

those with loathing thoughts
and deceiving eyes with reverent

prayer aim to hide the splintered
cross they so carefully prepare for

us. our futile knocks to be let in
are met with a most unwelcome

phrase telling us our skin is too
brown for this house of God. yet,

we wait quietly outside the gate
for Christ to come speaking of unity

in his foreign tongue and casting
a net of choice words at the assembly

seated inside with its confounded
notion of the divine. once more,

in this small corner of the earth
where Sunday wears a crown of

thorns the people behind the bolted
gate refuse to see, we shout woe to

you for building an unholy house
and spinning away from truth.

Twisted

the bell rings above
the altar that sits open

to the sky surrounded
by dead souls that jumble

words about the people
disfigured by inhospitable

words. the chalice held
high reeks of blood, bone

and people who never blush
when standing before God

in false confession. the ancient
scriptures twisted and raised

by sacerdotal hands signal
time to pass the collection

plate, and the good news
meant for the poor vaults

into another day of certain
darkness. history will not

blame us for not returning
to this narrow-minded place.